The Hope *of the* World

Discovering the Biblical Names of Jesus

JOEL OSTEEN

Contents

Alpha and Omega..4

Advocate..8

Author and Perfecter of Our Faith..12

Authority..16

Bread of Life..20

Beloved Son of God..24

Bridegroom..28

Chief Cornerstone..32

Deliverer..36

Good Shepherd..40

Great High Priest..44

Holy Servant..48

I Am..52

Immanuel..56

Judge..60

King of Kings..64

Lamb of God..68

Light of the World..72

Lion of the Tribe of Judah...76

Messiah...80

Prophet...84

Redeemer...88

The Resurrection and the Life..92

Rock..96

Savior..100

The Door..104

The Way..108

The Word..112

The True Vine..116

Truth...120

Wonderful Counselor, Mighty God,
Everlasting Father, Prince of Peace..................................124

Alpha & Omega

REVELATION 22:13, NIV

"I am the Alpha and the Omega, the First and the Last, the Beginning and the End."

The Bible opens with Genesis 1:1, "In the beginning God ..." God is the Alpha, the First, the Beginning.

Verses 1 and 14 in the first book of John go on to say that God is not just one, but three in one: *"the Word was with God, and the Word was God"* and *"the Word became flesh and dwelt among us"* (KJV). We know that Jesus is the Word — part of what we call the Trinity — who was there from the beginning (the Alpha) and who lived on the earth in human flesh.

The last chapter of the Bible is Revelation 22. It concludes that Jesus is coming soon, saying, *"... Amen. Come, Lord Jesus"* (v. 20). He will be there until it is finished — the Omega, the Last, the End.

"I am the Alpha and the Omega," says the Lord God, *"who is, and who was, and who is to come, the Almighty."*
Revelation 1:8, NIV

Jesus is — He's here and now.
Jesus was — He was there at the beginning.
And Jesus is to come — this life is not over until
He says it is, until He returns, until the end.

You can trust Jesus with your past, present, and future
because He is and was and will be here for all time. *"I am the
Alpha and the Omega, the First and the Last (the Before all
and the End of all)."* **Revelation 22:13, AMPC**

God knows how things work. He is the Alpha and the Omega, He is the beginning and the end, and He is everything in between. He is where you are right now, and in between it all."

—JOEL

Advocate

1 JOHN 2:1, AMP

My little children (believers, dear ones), I am writing you these things so that you will not sin and violate God's law. And if anyone sins, we have an Advocate [who will intercede for us] with the Father: Jesus Christ the righteous [the upright, the just One, who conforms to the Father's will in every way — purpose, thought, and action].

An advocate is someone who supports you, speaks up on your behalf, and defends your rights.

We often think of children needing advocates because they either don't know what is best for them or they don't know how to express their needs.

We, too, are like children, *"... babies who need milk and cannot eat solid food"* (Hebrews 5:12, NLT). We don't always know what is best for us. We don't always choose what is best for us. And we don't always have the words to defend ourselves against Satan, "the accuser" (see Revelation 12:10), especially when we know we *"have sinned and fall short of the glory of God"* (Romans 3:23, NIV).

But Jesus knows exactly what we need. He knows our hearts and intentions. He died in our place; therefore, He has the authority to go before God and advocate for us — to intercede, stand in place of our sins, defend, and plead our case — a case that, because of Him, has already been won.

God being for you is more than the world being against you.

—JOEL

thoughts

Author & Perfecter of Our Faith

HEBREWS 12:1–2, NASB

Therefore, since we have so great a cloud of witnesses surrounding us, let us also lay aside every encumbrance and the sin which so easily entangles us, and let us run with endurance the race that is set before us, fixing our eyes on Jesus, the author and perfecter of faith, who for the joy set before Him endured the cross, despising the shame, and has sat down at the right hand of the throne of God.

Someone once said that a writer becomes an author once a story is published.

Consider the Scripture that says Jesus is the "author and perfecter of faith." Jesus wrote your story long ago, before time even began. And when you came into existence, when you chose faith, He became the author and perfecter of it.

You can have faith, but to have living faith, Jesus must be part of it. You may think that your faith is the size of a mustard seed, or you may declare "I believe; help my unbelief!" But with Him, with our eyes fixed on Him, faith is made perfect. We choose a life of faith, and He perfects it as only the One who suffered on our behalf can.

For it was fitting for Him, for whom are all things, and through whom are all things, in bringing many sons to glory, to perfect the author of their salvation through sufferings. **Hebrews 2:10, NASB**

There's nothing more powerful than your faith. When you believe, when you expect things to change, when you live with expectancy, that's what activates God's power.

—JOEL

Authority

MATTHEW 28:18, AMP

Jesus came up and said to them,
"All authority (all power of absolute
rule) in heaven and on earth has
been given to Me."

There is a difference between power and authority.

Power is related to ability — the capacity to effect change. Authority relates to the rightful, sanctioned use of power. A random person with a gun has power. A uniformed police officer with a gun has both power and authority.

Throughout His life and ministry, Jesus displayed tremendous power — opening blind eyes, calming storms, and restoring the dead to life. And, in His words, He revealed and declared His God-given authority to use that power. Here is the truly stunning part of that revelation: Jesus then delegated His authority to His followers. That includes you.

As Luke 9:1 reveals: *"When Jesus had called the Twelve together, he gave them **power and authority** to drive out all demons and to cure diseases"* (NIV, emphasis added). When Jesus issued the Great Commission, He began by saying,

> *"All authority in heaven and on earth has been given to me. Therefore go and make disciples of all nations ..."* (Matthew 28:18–19, NIV).

Because you have the Holy Spirit, you have been given power. And because you are in Christ, you have His authority.

You are a person of destiny, equipped and empowered to accomplish all that God has called you to do.

—JOEL

Bread of Life

JOHN 6:35, NIV

Then Jesus declared, "I am the bread of life. Whoever comes to me will never go hungry, and whoever believes in me will never be thirsty."

It's natural to read Scripture passages about the "Bread of Life" and remember the Israelites and their journey out of Egypt into the Promised Land.

During their 40 years of wandering, God provided daily bread — manna from heaven — to sustain them. It was their source of life during that difficult season. Likewise, Jesus is our Source of Life. He is our Living Water. Our Daily Bread. Our Bread of Life. He assures us that if we come to Him, acknowledge Him, believe and accept Him, He will sustain us to the point where we will never hunger again — not only in this life but in the one to come (see John 6:33, 35, 51).

Interpreting this as a spiritual metaphor, theologian Blaise Pascal (1623–62) wrote:

"What else does this craving, and this helplessness, proclaim but that there was once in man a true happiness, of which all that now remains is the empty print and trace? This he tries in vain to fill with everything around him, seeking in things that are not there the help he cannot find in those that are, though none can help, since this infinite abyss can be filled only with an infinite and immutable object; in other words by God himself." (*Pensées*)

The "infinite abyss" that Pascal refers to is a God-shaped hole inside of us. We feel that emptiness or vacuum in our souls and try to alleviate it with worldly things — food, alcohol, busyness, recognition, social media — but as Pascal attests, that "infinite abyss" can only be filled by "God himself." Thus, coming to Jesus — believing, accepting, and receiving the Bread of Life — is the only way to truly satisfy the longing inside all of us.

"I am the Bread of Life [the Living Bread which gives and sustains life]." **John 6:48, AMP**

When you turn to the Creator, supernatural things happen. He wants to help you, to heal you, to free you, to increase you, to take you places that you've never dreamed of. He's longing to be good to you. Look to Him as your Source.

—JOEL

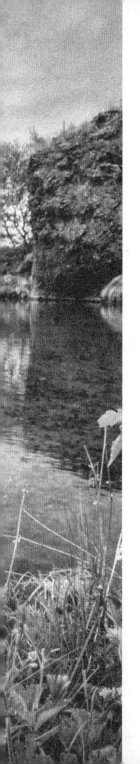

Beloved Son of God

MATTHEW 3:17, NKJV

And suddenly a voice came from heaven, saying, "This is My beloved Son, in whom I am well pleased."

John the Baptist must have looked like a wild man. His clothing was made of camel's hair. He ate locusts and honey.

He preached repentance while living in the wilderness. Yet people flocked to him to be baptized. They must have wondered, "Could he be the Son of God?" But John assured them: *"… He who is coming after me is mightier than I, and I am not fit to remove His sandals; He will baptize you with the Holy Spirit and fire"* (Matthew 3:11, NASB).

And then one day it happened: Jesus showed up! He came to John, and John immediately recognized Jesus for who He was — the beloved Son of God. Just as John, the baby, had leapt in Elizabeth's womb when Mary arrived at her doorstep, pregnant with Jesus, John, again, cried out at the sight of Jesus coming.

Jesus asked John to baptize Him, *"But John tried to prevent Him, saying, 'I have need to be baptized by You, and do You come to me?'"* (v. 14). John's argument that he shouldn't baptize Jesus, but that it should be the other way around, is similar to a later scene when Peter tried to prevent Jesus from washing his feet. In fact, both of these instances foreshadow Jesus' ministry in its entirety: Jesus defied all expectations, came to serve not to be served, and preached that the first would be last and the last would be first.

And so John baptized Jesus in the Jordan River. And if there was any doubt at all about who the real Son of God was, it was laid to rest as we read in Matthew 3:17 how when Jesus rose up from the water, the heavens opened up, a dove descended on Him, and the voice of God was heard, saying, *"This is my beloved Son ..."* (KJV).

For He received from God the Father honor and glory when such a voice came to Him from the Excellent Glory: "This is My beloved Son, in whom I am well pleased."
2 Peter 1:17, NKJV

When you serve others (as Jesus did), when you make somebody else's life better, when you lift up people, when you help heal those that are hurting, not only are they getting blessed, but you're getting blessed. You are being fed. You're getting filled back up.

—JOEL

Bridegroom

Jesus answered, "How can the guests of the bridegroom mourn while he is with them? The time will come when the bridegroom will be taken from them; then they will fast."

"Bridegroom" is another name for groom. In this passage, Jesus referred to Himself as the groom and His disciples as the bride.

The apostle Paul made a similar analogy in Ephesians 5 in which he referred to Christ as the groom and the Church as His bride. Considering that "bride" and "groom" are words typically reserved for the wedding day of two people, we can look at the entire life and ministry of Jesus on Earth as a wedding day — a day to celebrate, a festive day, a day of hope and joy, a day of vows and promises. In the passage in Matthew, the Pharisees argued that the disciples should be fasting, for this was a common religious practice in order to eliminate whatever separates you from God. But nothing stood between the disciples and God — Jesus was right there among them!

The Old Testament book, Song of Songs, is largely a loving poetic dialog between a bridegroom and his bride. The two main characters in this book clearly adore one another and praise each other lavishly. Biblical scholars have seen Song of Songs as a symbolic allegory of the love relationship between Jesus and His bride.

In Song of Songs 5:16, the bride declares of the bridegroom: *"His mouth is sweetness itself; he is altogether lovely. This is my beloved, this is my friend ..."* This is Jesus to us ... the One who adores us as a bridegroom adores his bride.

Let it get down in your spirit that God is looking at you with a smile on His face, and He loves you with an everlasting love!

—JOEL

Chief Cornerstone

PSALM 118:22, NASB

The stone which the builders rejected has become the chief corner stone.

Imagine a group of builders who were just setting out on a project and were creating two piles of stones: one pile included the stones to be used in the building project and the other pile was all of the rejected stones — the ones too flawed, irregular, soft, or different to be used.

Out of the "good" pile, they would obviously choose the most perfect stone to use as the chief cornerstone because it would lay the foundation of the structure and determine the placement of every other stone; every other move that would take place would be based on that stone.

Everyone thought they knew what Jesus would look like, be like, and know the rules He would follow and the ones He would strictly enforce. When Jesus showed up, many rejected Him. He wasn't what they expected. Instead of being hard, He was full of grace. Instead of being strict, He showed mercy. Instead of ruling with an iron fist, He drew in the sand with His fingertips and washed His disciples' feet. Instead of hanging out with the "who's who" of Israel, He hung out with fishermen, tax collectors, and little children. Many rejected Him; and yet, He was the one God had chosen. And God not only chose Him and placed Him in the "to-be-used" pile in the building of the kingdom, but He chose Him as the cornerstone — "the Chief Cornerstone" — the stone that all the foundations of the world would be built upon.

Consequently, you are no longer foreigners and strangers, but fellow citizens with God's people and also members of his household, built on the foundation of the apostles and prophets, with Christ Jesus himself as the chief cornerstone. In him the whole building is joined together and rises to become a holy temple in the Lord. And in him you too are being built together to become a dwelling in which God lives by his Spirit. **Ephesians 2:19–22, NIV**

God's grace is coming to you right now. God is saying, "I'm not mad at you. I'm madly in love with you. I'm not holding anything against you. I'm not keeping a record of your mistakes. I'm not even interested in your past. I'm interested in your future."

—JOEL

Deliverer

ROMANS 11:26, NIV

... As it is written: "The deliverer will come from Zion; he will turn godlessness away from Jacob."

Prior to the abolition of slavery in the United States, a form of music called African American spirituals emerged among the enslaved.

African slaves created songs to describe what it was like to be enslaved, but they also created songs of hope, as they looked forward to freedom — their own personal Promised Land of Canaan. These spirituals — this sense of hope — was greatly influenced by Scripture. They drew inspiration from popular biblical figures such as Daniel, Moses, and even Jesus. Hope came from the fact that, whether they were delivered from slavery in this life or in the heavenly realm, one way or another, Jesus would deliver them.

In a similar vein, Paul's letters to the Thessalonians were written during a time of great persecution. The church in Thessalonica faced tyranny and oppression. They were young in their faith, and Paul was determined to encourage them with his letters. So, he wrote of Jesus, "the Deliverer," knowing that they would receive encouragement and a sense of hope if they focused on the One who could deliver them from their persecutions.

As Paul reminds us in his letter to the Colossians: Through Christ, we have been delivered from the domain of darkness and transferred to the Kingdom of God's dear Son (see Colossians 1:13). Jesus has delivered us from the evil masters of selfishness, fear, oppression, and all of the curses of sin. We are free.

Don't try to figure everything out. That can just make you stressed and overwhelmed. Come back to a place of peace. In God's timing, you're going to be delivered. God is a trustworthy God.

—JOEL

JOHN 10:11, NIV

Good Shepherd

"I am the good shepherd. The good shepherd lays down his life for the sheep."

When you read the Bible, you might notice that God often repeats Himself. He does this for a reason.

Studies show that it takes anywhere from seven to seventeen times of repeating something for it to stick in our brain as a memory. In eighteen verses of John chapter 10, Jesus uses the analogy of the shepherd and His sheep; so we know it must be important — something He wants us to take hold of and remember.

What do we know about the Shepherd? The Shepherd is *"good"* (v. 11). He is *"the one who enters by the gate"* (v. 2), *"calls His own sheep by name"* (v. 3), *"goes on ahead of the sheep"* (v. 4), and *"lays down His life for the sheep"* (vv. 11–12). And what do we know about the sheep? The sheep know their Shepherd's voice and follow Him (see John 10:4, 14).

Why is it important to know the Shepherd's voice? Because there are imposters out there — thieves that come to *"steal and kill and destroy"* (v. 10) — but there is one

Shepherd (v. 16) who has come to give life, and to lay down His own life for His flock. When we know the Good Shepherd and His voice, when we follow Him, we are led in the way of everlasting protection, comfort, and peace.

Of all the things God wants us to remember about Jesus, the most important is that He is the Good Shepherd — the One who willingly laid down His life for us.

"I am the good shepherd; I know my sheep and my sheep know me." **John 10:14, NIV**

The Good Shepherd will fight your battles, He will lead you into green pastures and restore your soul. You may go through some valleys, some difficult times, but you don't have to fear any evil. For the Lord your God, the Good Shepherd, is with you.

—JOEL

Great High Priest

HEBREWS 4:14, NIV

Therefore, since we have a great high priest who has ascended into heaven, Jesus the Son of God, let us hold firmly to the faith we profess.

In the Old Testament, men were anointed to be priests over the people.

These priests were in charge of all things spiritual and all things related to God — including reminding the people of their sins and performing ritual animal sacrifices to ask God's forgiveness for their transgressions. The Old Testament high priest was the mediator between God and man.

But then Jesus came along — the "Great High Priest" whose name is above all names (see Philippians 2:9) and whose priesthood is permanent (see Hebrews 7:24). He turned things completely upside down. No longer are earthly priests necessary to remind us of our imperfections because we now have a Great High Priest who has been tempted, just like all of us, yet never transgressed. No longer are sacrificial offerings necessary to atone for our sins and appease God because Jesus, our Great High Priest, willingly became the ultimate sacrifice for us, interceding on our behalf.

Unlike the other high priests, he does not need to offer sacrifices day after day, first for his own sins, and then for the sins of the people. He sacrificed for their sins once for all when he offered himself. For the law appoints as high priests men in all their weakness; but the oath, which came after the law, appointed the Son, who has been made perfect forever. **Hebrews 7:27–28, NIV**

God is always at work in the life a believer. That's what the Word of God says, so just run into His presence. Don't walk. Don't stroll. Give it all you've got and run! Run into His presence!

—JOEL

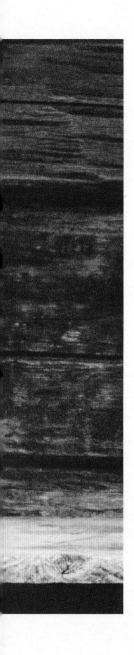

Holy Servant

ACTS 4:27, NLT

"In fact, this has happened here in this very city! For Herod Antipas, Pontius Pilate the governor, the Gentiles, and the people of Israel were all united against Jesus, your holy servant, whom you anointed."

Everyone — King Herod, Pontius Pilate, Jews, and Gentiles — were all united against Jesus, resulting in Jesus' crucifixion.

But even when everyone was against Him, Jesus remained firm in His faith — a Holy Servant of the one true God — committed to the plan that had been predestined before the beginning of the world.

Jesus declared that He did not come to do His own will but rather to fulfill the will of the Father (see John 6:38–46). And He modeled servanthood with humility and compassion.

In Acts 4, we read how Jesus' disciples were praying for the same fortitude and holy boldness that Jesus had, as they lifted their voices in prayer together. They cried out to God for the same strength, healing power, and courage that Jesus showed in the face of persecution. And God proved Himself faithful once again. The disciples repeatedly faced imprisonment and even death, yet they continued to preach the Word of God, empowered by the witness of the Holy Servant Jesus to speak truth and make disciples.

"And now, Lord, observe their threats [take them into account] and grant that Your bond-servants may declare Your message [of salvation] with great confidence, while You extend Your hand to heal, and signs and wonders (attesting miracles) take place through the name [and the authority and power] of Your holy Servant and Son Jesus."
Acts 4:29–30, AMP

You can't be good to somebody without God being good back to you. We don't do it for that reason. That's just the way God is. When you give, He gives you more back. When you show someone favor, He shows you more favor.

—JOEL

I Am

JOHN 8:58, NKJV

Jesus said to them, "Most assuredly, I say to you, before Abraham was, I AM."

Before caller ID or cell phones, if you answered the phone and the call was for someone else but you didn't recognize the voice on the other end of the line, you would ask who was calling.

In Exodus 3:13–14, in a familiar scene with a burning bush, Moses essentially asked the same question of God: "When I go to the Israelites and tell them I'm going to lead them out of Egypt, who should I say called me? Who should I say sent me? Who is this?" And God responded: *"I AM WHO I AM ..."* (Exodus 3:14, NKJV).

Jesus reminds us of this familiar scene in John 8:56–57 when, debating with the Pharisees, He claims to have existed before Abraham was even born. The Pharisees knew that wasn't possible — He wasn't even 50 years old. How could He have been alive 2,000 years ago? But Jesus wasn't claiming to physically live before Abraham was born; He was declaring His divinity — the Alpha and the Omega; the

One who was and is and is to come (see Revelation 1:8). To emphasize His point, Jesus claims the personal name of God, which was used when He spoke to Moses out of the burning bush: "I AM."

He is the same yesterday, today, and forever. His love is everlasting and His mercy inexhaustible.

It is good to stop and say, "I am blessed." You are a child of the Most High God. You were created in His image to do His good works. He has blessed you and crowned you with favor and honor.

—JOEL

Immanuel

ISAIAH 7:14, AMP

Therefore the Lord Himself will give you a sign: Listen carefully, the virgin will conceive and give birth to a son, and she will call his name Immanuel (God with us).

Isaiah spoke this prophecy to King Ahaz during the period of the kings and prophets.

God frequently gave the underdog king, Ahaz, victory in battle, but it took faith in the prophets and the Word of the Lord for the king to believe what he could not yet see. Isaiah told King Ahaz to ask God for a sign, but he refused, thinking that asking for a sign would be testing the Lord. Isaiah declared that *"the Lord Himself will give you a sign"* and speaks very clearly about the coming Messiah: *"... the virgin will conceive and give birth to a son, and she will call his name Immanuel (God with us)" (Isaiah 7:10-14, AMP).*

Matthew repeats this prophecy of Isaiah in his first chapter. Then he writes seventeen verses devoted to the lineage of Jesus. Matthew's audience was primarily Jewish believers who knew the prophecies of the Old Testament, so he regularly quoted from it to show them how Jesus fulfilled those prophecies. He used the lineage to show how Jesus was a descendant of David, from the "stump of Jesse." When an angel appeared to Joseph, the angel repeated Isaiah's prophecy to prove that Mary had not deceived Joseph but had conceived of the Holy Spirit. There was no need to stress over baby names because this one had been named long ago — Immanuel: God, here on Earth, walking and breathing, and living with us.

All this happened in order to fulfill what the Lord had spoken through the prophet [Isaiah]: "BEHOLD, THE VIRGIN SHALL BE WITH CHILD AND GIVE BIRTH TO A SON, AND THEY SHALL CALL HIS NAME IMMANUEL"— which, when translated, means, "GOD WITH US." **Matthew 1:22–23, AMP**

God never leaves us alone. We're never lacking. He is always with us.

—JOEL

Judge

ACTS 10:42, NLT

And he ordered us to preach everywhere and to testify that Jesus is the one appointed by God to be the judge of all — the living and the dead.

When Jesus is referred to as "Judge," it is in the context of His relationship to the Father.

In John 5 (NLT), Jesus explains that everything He does is a reflection of His Father — God shows mercy, so Jesus shows mercy. God raises from the dead, so Jesus raises from the dead. But when it comes to judgment, Jesus claims that this is His responsibility alone: *"In addition, the Father judges no one. Instead, He has given the Son absolute authority to judge ..."* (v. 22). Why? *"... So that everyone will honor the Son, just as they honor the Father ..."* (v. 23).

Jesus explains how He will judge: Very simply, those who listen will live and rise again and have eternal life and those who don't listen will experience judgment. Jesus also emphasizes that His judgement is just: *"I can do nothing on my own. I judge as God tells me. Therefore, my judgment is just, because I carry out the will of the one who sent me, not my own will"* (v. 30).

When He made this claim, Jesus was both perfect and human. As a human He experienced all the temptations we experience, including wanting others to pay for what they've done rather than showing them the same mercy we desire for ourselves. But because Jesus was acting out of the authority given to Him by the Father, He could set aside His human desires and act according to the will of God, thus making Him the only one capable of being fair, reasonable, and just in His office as Judge.

For those who reject God's gracious offer of forgiveness and reconciliation in Jesus, the prospect of one day standing before such a pure and holy judge will be a terrifying one. But those of us who have said yes to Him will come before Him with joy and expectancy, knowing we are clothed in the spotless robe of righteousness, which is His extraordinary gift to us.

Those enemies that have come against you: the enemy of sickness, the enemy of depression, of fear, lack, struggle ... Get ready! God is about to judge in your favor. He's about to overrule some things. What you're dealing with is not permanent. You're about to get a new verdict. God is about to turn some things around.

—JOEL

King of Kings

REVELATION 17:14, AMP

"They will wage war against the Lamb (Christ), and the Lamb will triumph and conquer them, because He is Lord of lords and King of kings, and those who are with Him and on His side are the called and chosen (elect) and faithful."

Everything that the people cried out to God for in the Old Testament — kings, prophets, judges, answers, and help — He gave them.

Yet, all the while, God knew that the ultimate King, the ultimate Prophet, the ultimate Judge, the ultimate Answer, the ultimate Help would come in His appointed time — the King of kings would come to reign over all.

Hierarchy was everything in the Old Testament (and continues today). There was a proper order, proper channels, a chain of command, and a delineation of authority in place at that time. Sons inherited their fathers' kingdoms. Brothers and mothers tricked or stole or murdered their way into the coveted seats. The transfer of power, when a father died, could completely change the course of the people's lives.

But there was One whom God knew from the beginning would be Lord over all — King of kings — the highest authority — Jesus.

Afterward the sons of Israel will return [in deep repentance] and seek the Lord their God and [seek from the line of] David their king [the King of kings — the Messiah]; and they will come trembling to the LORD and to His goodness and blessing in the last days.
Hosea 3:5, AMP

Give Jesus honor and praise today because He is the King of kings and the Lord of lords. He is the One who saves us, redeems us, and empowers us to move forward in Him.

—JOEL

Lamb of God

JOHN 1:29, NIV

The next day John saw Jesus coming toward him and said, "Look, the Lamb of God, who takes away the sin of the world!"

In the Old Testament, a Passover lamb was required as a sacrifice to remember the final plague that God sent against Pharaoh before the Israelites were freed from slavery.

On the night of that fateful plague, houses that had the blood of a lamb smeared on the doorposts would be spared. But houses that lacked the lamb's blood would be punished with the death of that household's firstborn son. After the Israelites were freed, God asked them to honor His sparing of their sons by sacrificing a lamb in remembrance of the Passover. That lamb was to be young, perfect, without blemish or defect.

We no longer have to practice this ritual sacrifice because the Lamb of God — Jesus — was the ultimate and final sacrifice. He was young. He was perfect. He was without sin or fault. And His blood was shed for our sins so that God's judgment would pass over us once and for all: *"but [you were actually purchased] with precious blood, like that of a [sacrificial] lamb unblemished and spotless, the priceless blood of Christ"* (1 Peter 1:19, AMP).

The Passover lamb, a reality of the Old Testament, was merely a foreshadowing of the Lamb of God — the ultimate sacrifice and the only One able to pay the price for our transgressions once and for all.

As Jesus walked by, John looked at him and declared, "Look! There is the Lamb of God!" **John 1:36, NLT**

Instead of accepting things that are holding you back, why don't you start saying, "Father, thank You that the blood of Your Son, Jesus, has cancelled out every bad seed in my life. Thank You that it's canceled out addiction, anger problems, a spirit of lack, and depression. Lord, thank You that I am free."

—JOEL

JOHN 8:12, NIV

Light of the World

When Jesus spoke again to the people, he said, "I am the light of the world. Whoever follows me will never walk in darkness, but will have the light of life."

Jesus spoke these words while standing in the temple treasury (see John 8:20).

This area of the temple was traditionally lit by candles to represent the pillar of fire that led the Israelites out of Egypt and through the wilderness: *"The LORD went ahead of them. He guided them during the day with a pillar of cloud, and he provided light at night with a pillar of fire. This allowed them to travel by day or by night"* (Exodus 13:21, NLT). The pillar of fire was a source of guidance, protection, and a promise that the presence of God was there with them as they escaped slavery in search of the Promised Land.

Jesus is that pillar of fire in our lives. As the Light of the World, He is present with us to guide, protect us from evil (darkness), and give life to us. But Jesus is clear: We must take action in order to have that source of light in our lives — we must choose to follow Him.

Just as we stumble in a dark room, we would stumble in this world without His light. And many, who have not chosen to walk with Him, do stumble.

The Word gave life to everything that was created, and his life brought light to everyone. The light shines in the darkness, and the darkness can never extinguish it. God sent a man, John the Baptist, to tell about the light so that everyone might believe because of his testimony. John himself was not the light; he was simply a witness to tell about the light. The one who is the true light, who gives light to everyone, was coming into the world. **John 1:4–9, NLT**

Jesus said, "Let your light shine before others, that they may see your good deeds" (Matthew 5:16, NIV). It doesn't say to let your light shine before people that deserve it, people that don't have any issues, people that have it all together. No, let your light shine before all people. How do you do it? By letting them see your good deeds.

—JOEL

Lion of the Tribe of Judah

REVELATION 5:5, NLT

But one of the twenty-four elders said to me, "Stop weeping! Look, the Lion of the tribe of Judah, the heir to David's throne, has won the victory. He is worthy to open the scroll and its seven seals."

In Genesis 49, the twelve sons of Israel (Jacob) gathered around their father to hear him prophesy of the days to come.

These twelve sons were the fathers of the twelve tribes of Israel, including the tribe of Judah — the line to which Jesus would be born.

Jacob went to his sons, from the oldest to the youngest, to reveal to them the future of their tribes. To Reuben, the firstborn, he revealed that even though the birthright of power should be his, it would not be because of his transgression with his father's wife. Next, to Simeon and Levi, Jacob said that because of their anger and violent tempers, they would be scattered throughout the land. And then it was Judah's turn.

The lion was the symbol of Judah's tribe (see Genesis 49:9), and Jacob refers here to Judah as a "lion's cub," a "lion," and then a "lioness" (NIV) — exemplifying different aspects of character: strong, brave, heir to the throne, fierce, protective, king above all others. To Judah, Jacob said,

"Judah, you are the one whom your brothers shall praise ... The scepter [of royalty] shall not depart from Judah, nor the ruler's staff from between his feet, until Shiloh [the Messiah, the Peaceful One] comes, and to Him shall be the obedience of the peoples" (Genesis 49:8, 10, AMP).

Jacob was declaring that Christ, the Messiah, would come from the line of Judah (the genealogy of which is laid out in Matthew 1). This is what John refers to in Revelation 5 when he calls Jesus "the Lion of the tribe of Judah," assuring the angel that finally there was one worthy to unroll the scroll and break the seven seals.

For it is evident that our Lord arose from Judah ...
Hebrews 7:14, NKJV

You may face situations where you don't like it, you don't understand it, it's not fair; but if you'll just keep doing the right thing, your breakthrough is on the way. When you obey God, miracles happen, healing is released, new doors will open, problems will turn around.

—JOEL

Messiah

JOHN 1:41, NIV

The first thing Andrew did was to find his brother Simon and tell him, "We have found the Messiah" (that is, the Christ).

Jesus is the Messiah, the "Anointed One" (see Daniel 9:25, AMP) — preordained before the foundation of the world to be the Prince of Peace, the King of kings, Christ Jesus our Lord.

Anointing with oil was a common practice in the Old Testament that symbolized the setting apart of someone or something for a specific duty. In Exodus, God told Moses to anoint his brother Aaron and Aaron's sons to the priesthood: *"And you shall take the anointing oil, pour it on his head, and anoint him ... The priesthood shall be theirs for a perpetual statute. So you shall consecrate Aaron and his sons"* (Exodus 29:7, 9, NKJV). Moses was also told to anoint the tabernacle, the altar, and the animal sacrifices.

Not only were priests anointed in those days, but also kings and prophets. The anointed ones of God were expected to rule, prophesy, and preach on God's behalf; and they were held in high respect for their positions. Even when King Saul chased David with the intent to kill him, David refused to take vengeance into his own hands against the one whom God had anointed to be king (see 1 Samuel 26:23).

Jesus was called the Messiah because He too was anointed of God. He was anointed to preach the Gospel (see Luke 4:18) and heal the sick (see Mark 6:13), and He was anointed with the power of the Holy Spirit to do good works (see Acts 10:38). Every other position that had been anointed before His coming — priest, king, prophet, sacrifice — Jesus came to fulfill.

All the people wondered in amazement, and said, "Could this be the Son of David (the Messiah)?" **Matthew 12:23, AMP**

You don't have to go through life doing everything on your own. You have an advantage. God has placed His anointing on you. The anointing is a divine empowerment. It enables you to do things that you could not do on your own. It will cause you to accomplish dreams, even though you didn't have the talent. It will give you wisdom beyond your years. It will help you overcome obstacles that look insurmountable.

—JOEL

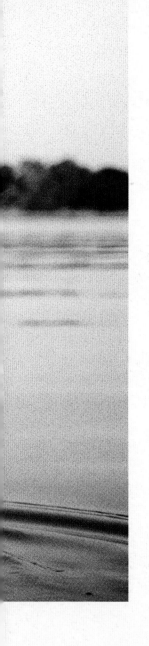

Prophet

MARK 6:4, NLT

Then Jesus told them, "A prophet is honored everywhere except in his own hometown and among his relatives and his own family."

Everywhere Jesus went, people flocked to Him to see the One they called a Prophet, the Messiah, the long-awaited One — that is, everywhere except His hometown of Nazareth.

There were only two things that amazed Jesus: faith and the lack of it. He could scarcely perform miracles in Nazareth because of the blatant unbelief of His former neighbors, relatives, and friends. If anyone should have believed in Him, shouldn't it have been the people closest to Him — the people who knew Him best? And yet that's often how it works. When something is part of your ordinary life, it is often easiest to overlook how extraordinary it really is.

To the people of Nazareth, Jesus was the boy next door. He was the son of a carpenter and of an ordinary girl. They'd seen Jesus playing in the streets with His brothers and sisters. They were there when He went missing at 12 years old and worried his parents sick because they couldn't find him anywhere. He may have been a good boy, but He was no prophet in their eyes. They certainly weren't going to waste their time believing in rumors that He could heal the sick, speak for God, or "set the captives free" (see Luke 4:18). In time, however, they would see how wrong they were, and they too would believe.

When Jesus entered Jerusalem, the whole city was stirred and asked, "Who is this?" The crowds answered, "This is Jesus, the prophet from Nazareth in Galilee." **Matthew 21:10–11, NIV**

If you're going to see something come to pass, you have to believe what you hear in your spirit and not what you see with your eyes. People may tell you that you'll never get well. You'll never get out of debt, never meet the right person, never accomplish your dreams. But if you listen, you'll hear a voice saying, "Healing is coming; you will lend and not borrow. New doors are about to open." Don't let what you see talk you out of what you've heard.

—JOEL

Redeemer

PSALM 19:14, NKJV

Let the words of my mouth and the meditation of my heart be acceptable in Your sight, O LORD, my strength and my Redeemer.

The book of Ruth is just four chapters long, but it speaks volumes about Jesus.

Ruth was a widow who chose to follow her mother-in-law, Naomi, rather than return home to her own family after her husband's death. Naomi had also lost her husband and both sons. She was bitter, with seemingly no hope to carry on her family line or take possession of the land that had once belonged to her husband. But she knew of a relative on her husband's side — a man named Boaz. So Naomi encouraged Ruth to seek him out. Ruth gleaned wheat from his fields, and when Boaz proved that he would be good to her, Naomi encouraged Ruth to approach him on the threshing floor —

more or less proposing marriage to him. Naomi knew that Boaz, as a close family member, had the power to redeem the family.

To redeem means to "buy back." In other words, Boaz could buy back their standing in the community and the land that had belonged to her husband. They could go from nothing to something, from death to life, from bitter to blessed once again.

Likewise, Jesus is our Kinsman-redeemer. He is the Bridegroom, and we are the bride. Evil came into the world to steal everything that God had planned for us, but Jesus came to buy it all back, restoring to us what is rightfully ours as heirs to the throne of God.

For I know that my Redeemer lives, and He shall stand at last on the earth. **Job 19:25, NKJV**

You may have gone through a loss or disappointment. You're hurting, but this is not how your story ends. God sees, and He's not only going to help you through, but He's going to fill your mouth with laughter. There's great joy in your future. The right people are already headed your way — new relationships, favor like you've never seen. Now, like Job, keep thanking God for what He said. Keep declaring, "My Redeemer lives."

—JOEL

The Resurrection and the Life

JOHN 11:25, NKJV

Jesus said to her, "I am the resurrection and the life. He who believes in Me, though he may die, he shall live."

Jesus spoke those words to Martha after her brother Lazarus had died.

Mary and Martha had sent for Jesus when their brother fell ill, but Jesus did not immediately come. In hindsight, we see that Jesus was not being rude, inconsiderate, or uncaring. In fact, He wept when He learned that Lazarus had died while He was on his way to him. Yet His delay was on purpose. Lazarus' death was necessary so that Jesus could perform the miracle of bringing him back to life — a foreshadowing of His own death and resurrection and a promise that, though we will all die one day, in Him there is resurrection and life.

Paul revealed Jesus as a "second Adam." Death came into the world when Adam, the first human, sinned in the Garden of Eden. Therefore, it makes sense that the resurrection of the dead would also come by man: *"For just as in Adam all die, so also in Christ all will be made alive"* (1 Corinthians 15:22, AMP). We die to our sin when we become joined to Christ, and we are raised to a new life through believing in Him. He truly is the Resurrection and the Life.

Therefore if you have been raised with Christ [to a new life, sharing in His resurrection from the dead], keep seeking the things that are above, where Christ is, seated at the right hand of God. **Colossians 3:1, AMP**

It may be Friday in your life right now. It looks kind of dark. You're not seeing good breaks. Business is slow. The medical report hasn't improved. My encouragement is, don't get stuck on Friday. Sunday is coming! Get ready for God to do something new. Your story doesn't end in defeat. It ends in victory!

—JOEL

Rock

1 CORINTHIANS 10:3-4, NIV

They all ate the same spiritual food and drank the same spiritual drink; for they drank from the spiritual rock that accompanied them, and that rock was Christ.

Paul warned the Corinthians that they were in danger of traveling the same road as their ancestors, the Israelites (whom God led out of Egypt).

Even though Jesus had traveled with the Israelites as the "spiritual rock that accompanied them," they still grumbled and complained and pleaded to turn back. The same temptation was true for the Corinthians: Even though they knew people who had physically seen and walked with Jesus, people who had been healed by Jesus, and those that had seen Jesus after His resurrection, they still were tempted to fall away. And the same is true for us.

We can open our hearts to Jesus, we can see Him work in our lives and the lives of others, and still doubt. But regardless of whether our hearts or minds waver, He never does. He is the Rock — firm and immovable (see Psalm 19:14, AMP). And His love for us never changes.

No one is holy like the LORD! There is no one besides you; there is no Rock like our God. **1 Samuel 2:2, NLT**

The enemy doesn't have the final say; God does. He says because your house is built on the rock, when it's all said and done, you won't be the victim. You will be the victor. You will still be standing, in Jesus' name.

—JOEL

Savior

LUKE 2:11, NKJV

For there is born to you this day in the city of David a Savior, who is Christ the Lord.

To become a Christian is to accept Jesus Christ as your personal Lord and Savior.

Acts 4:12 (NIV) says, *"Salvation is found in no one else, for there is no other name under heaven given to mankind by which we must be saved."* There is only one name under which we can be saved, under which we receive salvation: Jesus, our Savior.

Whoever believes and has decided to trust in Him [as personal Savior and Lord] is not judged [for this one, there is no judgment, no rejection, no condemnation]; but the one who does not believe [and has decided to reject Him as personal Savior and Lord] is judged already [that one has been convicted and sentenced], because he has not believed and trusted in the name of the [One and] only begotten Son of God [the One who is truly unique, the only One of His kind, the One who alone can save him].
John 3:18, AMP

We know that *"all have sinned and fall short of the glory of God"* (Romans 3:23, NASB) and all are in need of a Savior. But there is only One who can bring deliverance, redemption, and healing to ALL people: Jesus, our Savior, *"who wants all people to be saved and to come to a knowledge of the truth"* (1 Timothy 2:4, NIV).

The entire Bible is a testament that Jesus is the fulfillment of the promises of God. Jesus is the One who came into the world, died, and conquered death so that through him ALL people would have the opportunity to be saved.

But when the kindness of God our Savior and His love for mankind appeared, He saved us ... **Titus 3:4–5a, NASB**

"Lord Jesus, thank You for all that You've done for us. We all have a testimony of times that You protected us, favored us, saved us, and delivered us. You have brought great people into our lives. You've given us opportunities and talents. We recognize it all comes from You, our Father in Heaven above! Amen."

—JOEL

The Door

JOHN 10:9, AMP

I am the Door; anyone who enters through Me will be saved [and will live forever], and will go in and out [freely], and find pasture (spiritual security).

Several popular game shows, from *Let's Make a Deal* to *The Price Is Right*, invited contestants to play a game for a grand prize that was hidden behind one of three doors.

The challenge is for you to blindly pick a door. If you choose incorrectly, you may end up with a decent prize, or no prize at all, but only one door leads to the grand prize. This game is so popular that studies have been done to determine the odds and probability of choosing the correct door the first time and whether or not, given another chance, the odds are in your favor to change your choice if the doors are narrowed down to two.

In John 10:9, Jesus says He is "the Door" — the one and only door that leads to the grand prize: eternal life. You can try other doors. Other doors may make you happy for a little while, but only through one door — "the Door" — will you be saved.

Jesus relates our passage through the door to that of sheep: "... *'I assure you and most solemnly say to you, I am the Door for the sheep [leading to life]'"* (John 10:7, AMP). Through the wrong door, a sheep might find a wolf waiting to eat him, or a barren field, without sustenance. But through "the Door," a sheep will "find good pastures" (v. 9, NLT).

Jesus said, *"... I came that they may have and enjoy life, and have it in abundance [to the full, till it overflows]"* (John 10:10, AMP). That is the life you are 100 percent guaranteed to have when you find "the Door": Jesus.

God is called El Shaddai, the God of more than enough. Not the God of barely enough. Not the God of just-help-me-to-make-it-through, just live off the leftovers. No, He's the God of abundance, the God of overflow.

—JOEL

The Way

JOHN 14:6, AMP

Jesus said to him, "I am the [only] Way [to God] and the [real] Truth and the [real] Life; no one comes to the Father but through Me."

Robert Frost (1874–1963) is famous for having written a poem called "The Road Not Taken."

The poem begins with the line: "Two roads diverged in a yellow wood." There is a Scripture passage — Matthew 7:13–14 — that also speaks of two divergent paths: one through a narrow gate and one that is broad.

In both the Scripture and the poem, the traveler is forced to make a choice. In the poem, the character is sorry he can't go down both paths and spends a long time trying to see as far down each path as he can before he makes his decision. Unlike the poem, the Scripture passage tells us exactly what lies ahead: the broad path is described as "easy" but leading to "destruction"; while the narrow path is "difficult" yet leads to "everlasting life." While both paths in the poem are equally traveled, the narrow path in Scripture is clearly the road less traveled (see Matthew 7:14).

The narrator of Frost's poem imagines that someday he will spin the story of this fork in the road, claiming to have taken "the one less traveled," which has "made all the difference" in his life. Unlike the narrator of the poem, who assumes he'll never actually know whether or not this is true because he doubts he'll ever make it back to see where the other road leads, the Scripture describes a choice that truly is life-changing. We don't have to travel both roads to know where they lead. Scripture is clear: There is only one way to life — the narrow way — Jesus.

"Enter by the narrow gate; for wide is the gate and broad is the way that leads to destruction, and there are many who go in by it. Because narrow is the gate and difficult is the way which leads to life, and there are few who find it."
Matthew 7:13–14, NKJV

This is the day the Lord has made! Let's make a choice to rejoice, to be glad. Once we live this day, we can't get it back. Life is precious. We have to make the choice and say, "God, I'm not going to let somebody else take my joy. I'm going to be happy. I'm going to live this day in faith. I'm going to be good to somebody else. I'm going to love the people in my life."

—JOEL

The Word

JOHN 1:1 AMP

*In the beginning [before all time]
was the Word (Christ), and the
Word was with God, and the Word
was God Himself.*

The apostle John was the writer of the Gospel of John and Revelation.

In both books he referred to Jesus as "the Word."
In John 1:14 (AMP):

"And the Word (Christ) became flesh, and lived among us; and we [actually] saw His glory, glory as belongs to the [One and] only begotten Son of the Father, [the Son who is truly unique, the only One of His kind, who is] full of grace and truth (absolutely free of deception)."

And in Revelation 19:13 (NASB):

"He is clothed with a robe dipped in blood, and His name is called The Word of God."

Jesus is the "Word made flesh" — He is God, living, breathing, walking, and teaching here on Earth. And that "Word made flesh" is "clothed with a robe dipped in blood," signifying that He is the final sacrifice that covers the sins of all humanity.

When God created the heavens and the earth and everything in it, He spoke them into existence. Light, dark, water, land, vegetation, animals, man ... they are all the words of God made manifest. In the same manner, Jesus is "the Word" — He is God made manifest, and the ultimate fulfillment of God's divine plan.

It's so important to get in a habit of speaking victory over your life. All through the day, declare positive words: "I am blessed, I am strong, I am healthy, I'm surrounded by favor, something good is going to happen to me." The fruit of those words are blessings, favor, abundance. It's not enough to just think it. We give life to our faith by speaking it out.

—JOEL

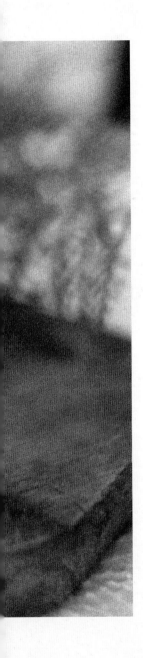

The True Vine

JOHN 15:1, NASB

"I am the true vine, and My Father is the vinedresser."

When Jesus spoke of being the vine, and God being the vinedresser (or "gardener"), He is not only telling us about His relationship with the Father, but He goes on to tell us about our relationship to Him.

As the vine, Jesus is the source. As the vinedresser, God is the caretaker, the watchful eye that ensures that the vine stays healthy: *"Every branch in Me that does not bear fruit, He takes away; and every branch that bears fruit, He prunes it so that it may bear more fruit"* (John 15:2, NASB). We are the branches. If we aren't bearing fruit — living up to our potential, growing in our relationship with Jesus, receiving from the Source — God will do what is necessary: He will prune, or cut off, those attitudes or harmful beliefs in us that prevent a fruitful life.

"'... As the branch cannot bear fruit of itself unless it abides in the vine, so neither can you unless you abide in Me'" (v. 4). A branch cannot live without being attached to a root. The same is true for us: without a connection to the True Vine, there is no way we can flourish.

"I am the vine, you are the branches; he who abides in Me and I in him, he bears much fruit, for apart from Me you can do nothing." **John 15:5, NASB**

What is the fruit we are called to bear — the fruit that flourishes when we are attached to the True Vine? According to Galatians 5:22–23, *"the fruit of the Spirit is love, joy, peace, forbearance, kindness, goodness, faithfulness, gentleness and self-control ..."* (NIV). God is glorified when we stay in close connection to the True Vine, and in doing so, we bear much fruit.

Every morning, it's good to admit your dependence on Him. "God, I need You today. I'm going to stay connected to the vine. I'm going to do my best, use my talents, work hard, but God I'm trusting You to bring the increase. I know apart from You I can do nothing."

—JOEL

Truth

JOHN 8:32, NASB

*"... and you will know the truth, and
the truth will make you free."*

When Jesus spoke these words to the Jewish people, they were confused.

They were descendants of Abraham, who had led the Israelites out of slavery and into the Promised Land. Therefore, they assumed that they were already free. What did they have to be freed from?

Jesus told them that anyone who sins is a slave to sin. Sin controls us by taking over our thoughts, hearts, attitudes, and actions; not unlike the way a master controls his slaves. Therefore, we are incapable of walking in freedom when we are burdened by sin. But there is a solution:

"For God made Christ, who never sinned, to be the offering for our sin, so that we could be made right with God through Christ" (2 Corinthians 5:21, NLT).

"So if the Son sets you free, you will be free indeed."
John 8:36, NIV

Why is freedom found only in Christ? Because He is the Truth, and John 8:32 tells us that the Truth will make us free. When you believe, walk in, and know the Truth [Jesus], you are truly free.

How can we trust that Jesus is Truth? Jesus is Truth because He comes from God, is seated at the right hand of God, and is God. And we know from Scripture that God is incapable of lying:

> *"God is not human, that he should lie, not a human being, that he should change his mind. Does he speak and then not act? Does he promise and not fulfill?"* (Numbers 23:19, NIV).

Believe, receive, and walk in the light of His Word today. His words are full of the Spirit and life (see John 6:63).

When we begin to align ourselves with God's truth, it's amazing the power that is released from us. That power is actually faith! We may not be able to change the circumstances, but Almighty God can!

—JOEL

Wonderful Counselor, Mighty God, Everlasting Father, Prince of Peace

For to us a child is born, to us a son is given, and the government will be on his shoulders. And he will be called Wonderful Counselor, Mighty God, Everlasting Father, Prince of Peace.

Isaiah spoke with anticipation about a child who would come, a child whose very nature would be wonderful, wise, peaceful, powerful, and everlasting.

Jesus is our Wonderful Counselor. In biblical times, He provided counsel to all who came to Him, counsel that left many awed and in wonder at His authority and wisdom. We are still able to go to Jesus for wise counsel today, seeking His will and wisdom in all that we do.

Jesus is our Mighty God: "'Then you will know that I, the LORD, am your Savior, your Redeemer, the Mighty One of Jacob'" (Isaiah 60:16, NASB). He is our hero. He is strong and powerful — mighty, to rule over the kingdom of darkness; yet, merciful, to intercede between us and God as the propitiation for our sins.

Jesus is the everlasting Father. He was and is and is to come — eternally. He was with the Father from the beginning and will be there at the end to bring forth the resurrection of the dead. He is our "Abba" father, with kindness and compassion, interest and direction, and love for all.

Jesus is the Prince of Peace: *"For he himself is our peace ..."* (Ephesians 2:14, NASB). Isaiah's prophecy, that a child would be born who would be called the Prince of Peace, was spoken during a time of war when God was seen as the One who would bring victory. But Jesus' reign ushered in a time of peace, and He was the Prince of it:

> *"For God in all his fullness was pleased to live in Christ, and through him God reconciled every-thing to himself. He made peace with everything in heaven and on earth by means of Christ's blood on the cross"* (Colossians 1:19–20, NLT).

Jesus is wise, powerful, eternal, and peaceful. His nature is wonderful. We know that full well.

God has something awesome in store for you. He would not have brought you this far to leave you. He's got fresh victory, fresh favor, fresh new anointing for you. Take the limits off of God, and watch what He is going to do! He's going to exceed your expectations!

—JOEL

Created and assembled for Joel Osteen Ministries by
Breakfast for Seven
2150 E. Continental Blvd., Southlake, TX 76092
breakfastforseven.com

Printed in China.

ISBN:978-1-951701-28-4